HUNGARY

Keith Lye

General Editor
Henry Pluckrose

Franklin Watts
London   New York   Sydney   Toronto

Facts about Hungary

Area:
93,030 sq. km.
(35,919 sq. miles)

Population:
10,796,000 (1986 estimate)

Capital:
Budapest

Largest cities:
Budapest (2,067,000)
Miskolc (210,000)
Debrecen (198,000)
Szeged (174,000)
Pécs (173,000)

Official language:
Hungarian (Magyar)

Religion:
Christianity

Main exports:
Machinery, industrial products, bauxite and aluminium, food

Currency:
Forint

Franklin Watts Limited
12a Golden Square
London W1

ISBN: UK Edition 0 86313 337 1
ISBN: US Edition 0 531 10105 3
Library of Congress Catalog
Card No: 85 51580

© Franklin Watts Limited 1986

Typeset by Ace Filmsetting Ltd,
Frome, Somerset
Printed in Hong Kong

Maps: Tony Payne
Design: Arthur Brown
Stamps: Stanley Gibbons Limited
Photographs: Zefa; Danube Travel, 4, 6, 7, 11, 12, 15, 17, 23, 25, 30, 31; Paul Forrester, 8; Frank Spooner Pictures 14
Front cover: Zefa
Back cover: Danube Travel

Hungary is a country in Eastern Europe. It is about the same size as Portugal. Hungary has no coastline. Its main outlet to the sea is the River Danube, seen here flowing through the capital, Budapest, on its way to the Black Sea.

A fertile plain called the Great Alföld covers more than half of Hungary. It lies east of the Danube. Horse rearing and training wild horses were once major activities. Here a Hungarian horseman, called a csikos, shows his skill at a horse show.

Western Hungary has some beautiful hilly regions, such as here in the Zala county in the southwest, and the forested Bakony ridge. A plain called the Little Alföld is in the northwest. The Little Alföld is another fertile farming region.

Hungary's only mountains are in the northeast. The highest peak is Mount Kékes, which is 1,015 metres (3,330 ft) high. These low mountains contain many resorts and skiing is popular in winter. Hungary has cold winters, but the summers are hot.

The shores around Lake Balaton, central Europe's largest lake, are dotted with resorts. At the resort of Tihany is an old Abbey, whose crypt is 900 years old. Christianity was introduced into Hungary in the late tenth century.

The picture shows some stamps and money used in Hungary. The main unit of currency is the forint, which is divided into 100 fillér.

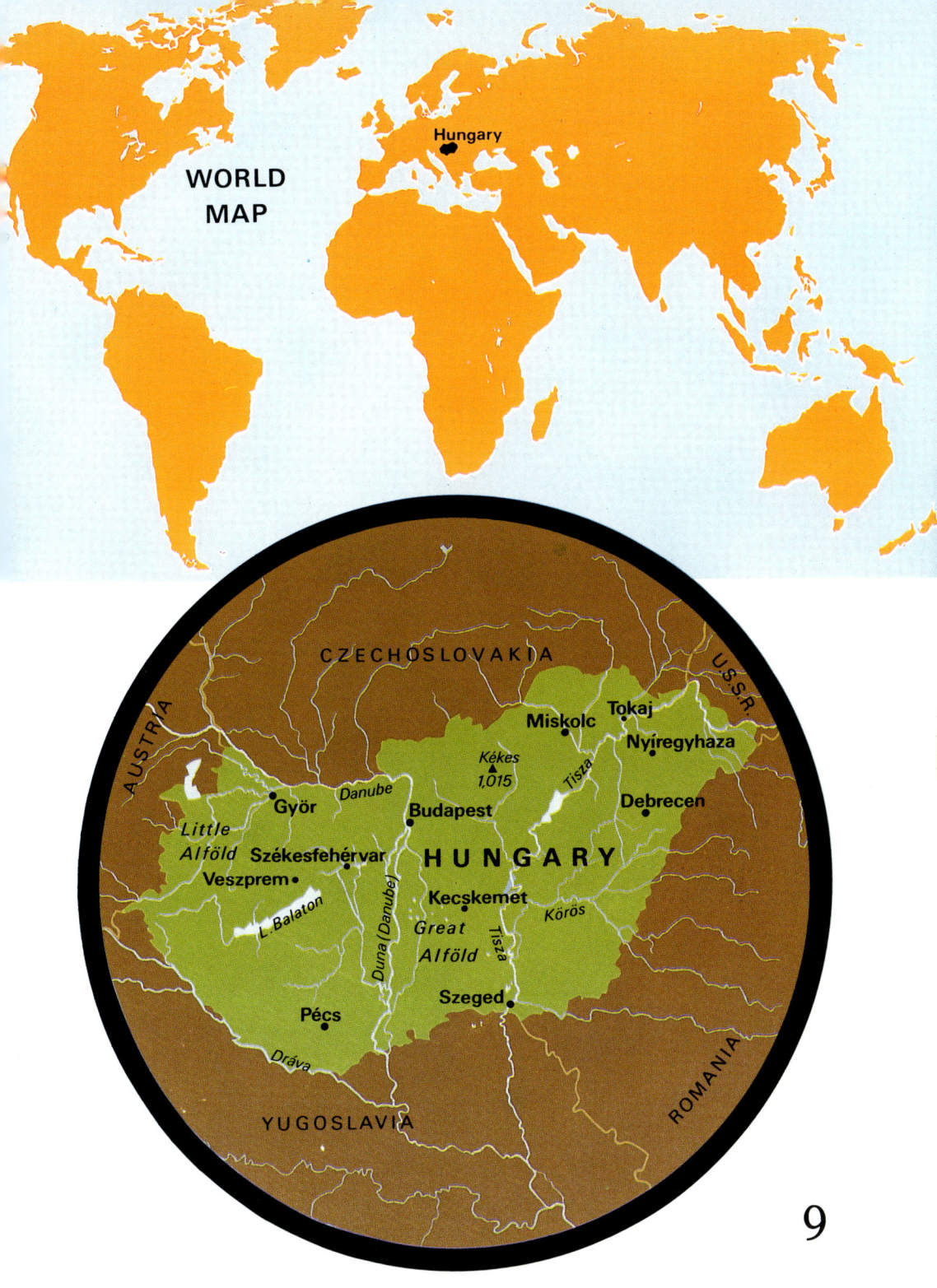

This bronze statue of St. Stephen on horseback is in Budapest. St. Stephen was Hungary's first king. He was crowned in AD 1001. He converted the Hungarians to Roman Catholicism.

The Crown of St. Stephen can be seen in Budapest's National Museum. The Turks conquered the kingdom of Hungary in the sixteenth century. They ruled what is now eastern and central Hungary. In the late seventeenth century, Austria seized all of Hungary.

In 1848, Lajos Kossuth, a Hungarian national hero, led a revolt against Austrian rule. He was defeated, but in 1867 Hungary was made a partner in the Austro-Hungarian Empire. This empire was defeated in World War I. The picture shows a statue of Lajos Kossuth in Budapest.

Hungary's Parliament stands on the Danube in Budapest. Its dome is capped by a red star. Hungary is a People's Republic. The Hungarian Socialist Workers' (or Communist) Party rules the country. In 1956, many Hungarians revolted against Communist rule, but Russian forces put down the revolt.

Hungary's armed forces form part of a military alliance called the Warsaw Pact. Hungary's allies include the Communist countries of Bulgaria, Czechoslovakia, East Germany, Poland, Romania and the USSR. Because of this alliance, Russian troops are stationed in Hungary.

In summer, Hungarians enjoy meals in outdoor restaurants. This picture was taken in Szeged, which is an important city in southeastern Hungary. About 55 out of every 100 Hungarians live in cities and towns.

Székesfehérvár is an ancient town in western Hungary. St. Stephen built its first cathedral and royal palace. Hungarian kings were crowned and many were buried here between the eleventh and sixteenth centuries.

St. Stephen's Basilica in Budapest was built in the nineteenth century. Half of the people of Hungary are Roman Catholics. Nearly one-fifth are Calvinists. There are other Protestant groups, some Orthodox Christians and some Jews.

Farmland covers about two-thirds of Hungary and farming employs 21 out of every 100 workers. Cereals are the most important crops. The picture shows the harvesting of flax. Flax is used to make rope and thread. Its seeds are used to make linseed oil.

Animal products acount for two-fifths of the value of farm products. Only one-twentieth of Hungary's farmland is privately owned. The rest is divided into collective farms, where people share the produce, and state farms, where workers get wages. On collective farms, families own small plots of land. Anything they produce here belongs to them.

Hungary is known for its wines. This vineyard is in the hills above Lake Balaton. A red wine called Bull's Blood is produced around Eger in the northeast. Tokaj, east of Miskolc, produces a famous sweet wine, which is called Tokaj.

Industry is Hungary's chief activity. It employs 43 out of every 100 workers. Bauxite, coal and oil are mined. Chemicals, steel and many metal goods are manufactured. Large industrial areas surround Budapest. Most industries are owned by the government.

Hungary has many light industries, such as glassmaking. There are also many small factories that produce such things as textiles, clothing and food. Hungarians are known for their inventiveness. The Rubik cube was invented by a Hungarian, Ernö Rubik.

Pottery is an ancient craft industry. The earliest Hungarian pottery dates back to the ninth century and the art of making pottery still flourishes. This large vase is being decorated in a small factory in the city of Pécs.

Ludwig van Beethoven, the great German composer, often stayed at the Brunswick Palace in Martonvásár, between Székesfehérvár and Budapest. It was here that Beethoven composed his famous "Moonlight" sonata.

Beethoven memorial concerts are held at Martonvásár every June and July. A bust of the composer can be seen behind the orchestra. Hungarians enjoy music. Their composers include Franz Liszt, Béla Bartók and Zoltán Kodály.

Elementary education is compulsory between the ages of 6 and 14. Some children then go to high schools that give a general education. Vocational schools offer special courses in farming, commerce and industry.

All the elementary schools and most secondary schools are run by the government. They provide free education. Hungary also has some independent schools run by religious groups. These schools charge a fee.

About 95 out of every 100 Hungarians are Magyars – the descendants of tribes from the east who entered Hungary in the late ninth century. There are also people of German, Slovak, Croat, Serb, Gypsy and Romanian origin. The picture shows typical Magyar village houses.

Hungarians like spicy food. They use a hot seasoning called paprika in many dishes, including a famous thick stew called goulash. Goulash, which can be a meal in itself, also contains meat, green peppers, onions, tomatoes, small dumplings and potatoes.

In summer, the shores of Lake Balaton are crowded with visitors. Wind surfing, sailing, swimming and water skiing are popular activities. Many tourists come from other Communist countries, such as Czechoslovakia and East Germany.

Hungarians love their traditions and their exciting folk music, often played by skilled violinists. Folk dances are performed on special occasions, such as holidays and weddings. Hungary has several professional folk dance companies.

Index

Balaton, Lake 7, 20, 30
Beethoven, Ludwig van
 24–25
Brunswick Palace 24
Budapest 3, 10–13, 17

Christianity 7, 10, 17, 21
Climate 6
Communism 13–14

Danube, River 3, 13

Education 26–27

Farming 18–20
Flax 18
Folk dances 31
Food 29

Glass making 22
Goulash 29
Government 13
Great Alföld 4

History 7, 10–14
Horses 4

Industry 21–23

Kékes, Mount 6
Kossuth, Lajos 12

Little Alföld 5

Magyars 28
Martonvásár 24–25
Money 8
Music 24–25, 31

Paprika 29
Pécs 23
Pottery 23

Religion 7, 10, 17, 27
Rubik cube 22

St. Stephen 10–11, 16–17
Schools 26–27
Skiing 6
Sports 6, 30
Stamps 8
Szeged 15
Székesfehérvár 16

Tihany 7

Warsaw Pact 14
Wind surfing 30
Wines 20

Zala 5